ROBOTICS™

ROBOTS THROUGH HISTORY

JERI FREEDMAN

rosen publishing's
rosen
central®

NEW YORK

Published in 2011 by The Rosen Publishing Group, Inc.
29 East 21st Street, New York, NY 10010

Copyright © 2011 by The Rosen Publishing Group, Inc.

First Edition

Library of Congress Cataloging-in-Publication Data

Freedman, Jeri.
Robots through history / Jeri Freedman.
    p. cm. — (Robotics)
Includes bibliographical references and index.
ISBN 978-1-4488-1236-3 (library binding)
ISBN 978-1-4488-2250-8 (pbk.)
ISBN 978-1-4488-2257-7 (6-pack)
1. Robotics–History–Juvenile literature. 2. Robots–History–Juvenile literature. I. Title.
TJ211.2.F74 2011
629.8'9209–dc22

                                                    2010024139

Manufactured in the United States of America

CPSIA Compliance Information: Batch #W11YA: For further information, contact Rosen Publishing, New York, New York, at 1-800-237-9932.

On the cover: Robots replace humans on the assembly line in a car manufacturing plant.

CONTENTS

INTRODUCTION

he Oxford American Dictionary defines a robot as "a machine capable of carrying out a complex series of actions automatically, especially one programmed by a computer." In other words, a robot is a machine that can be given instructions to perform physical tasks without human intervention. Today's robots are usually programmable machines— that is, their behavior can be controlled by changing the instructions they are given. Robotics is the science of robots and encompasses three main areas: mechanics, electronics, and software. This book examines the history of all three of these areas as they relate to robots.

Throughout history people have pursued the idea of creating artificial humans who would perform the same tasks as real people. Often, these artificial humans were conceived as machines that would perform labor in place of real people. In fact, the term "robot" was coined in 1920 by Czech writer Karel Čapek, who wrote a play called *R.U.R.* (which stands for Rossum's Universal Robots), which deals with artificial people created in a factory. Čapek credited his brother Joseph with coming up with the term "robot." The word "robot" is derived from the Czech word *robota*, which refers to forced labor performed by serfs (people in servitude to a feudal lord). Today, in factories around the world, many manufacturing tasks once performed by human laborers are now performed by industrial robots.

Robots can be stationary, like those that assemble products on an assembly line, or mobile like the Mars rover, scouting the terrain of remote locations. Some of the most fascinating robots are those that mimic life—whether they are robotic insects designed in a Massachusetts Institute of Technology (MIT) lab, or humanoid robots created by Honda's Japanese research lab.

Robots have been and are being developed for many purposes. There are robots designed for entertainment purposes (such as robotic pets), as well as robots created for serious scientific investigation in environments too hostile for scientists to examine first-hand. This book explores the attempts to design robots from earliest times to the present day, illustrating how various developments along the way contributed to our understanding of robotics and the technology we enjoy today.

CHAPTER 1
The Earliest Robots

The basic mechanical principles that allowed the development of automated machines and robotlike mechanisms were laid down well before modern times. The ancient Greeks were especially skilled at creating mechanical devices. Ancient Greek texts provide a record of a number of automated machines, including construction cranes, catapults, and water clocks with moving figures produced by Ctesibius (ca. third century BCE).

In the third century BCE, a work called *Mechanics* was written in Greece. It is attributed to the philosopher Aristotle (384–322 BCE). *Mechanics* describes a number of devices that are key to automating machines: levers, rollers, and gears; simple and compound pulleys; and other mechanical components. These basic devices are still used today in machines. Archimedes (287–212 BCE), another Greek philosopher interested in engineering, invented the worm gear. A worm gear is basically a cylinder of metal with grooves like those in a screw that interlocks with a conventional round, toothed gear and turns it. Among other advantages, this type of gear allows small, normally weak motors to produce more force to manipulate appendages on a

Figures and devices that move on their own mechanically are called automata. This is from the Greek word *automaton,* which means "self-acting" or "self-operating." Automata were used in the theater as far back as ancient Greece. In his work on automata, Hero of Alexandria (10–70 CE) recorded a number of automata used in theatrical and religious presentations, including moving figures and devices that produced sounds and flames. In the first century BCE, the Roman engineer Vitruvius recorded several automata as well.

All of these early automated devices relied on pulleys, pumps, pistons, gears, and levers to produce motion. Although today's robotic machines are controlled by electronic rather than mechanical means, the moving parts still consist of these

The use of construction cranes in the rebuilding of the city of Troy in this illustration by Jean Colombe shows that people of the Renaissance were familiar with pre-robotic machines.

types of mechanical components. A controller is a device that manages the overall movement of the parts of a mechanical or electronic device. Early controllers were mechanical. For example, a windup mechanism that turns gears that move a figure's arms and legs is a mechanical controller. An electronic controller does the same thing for modern robots, but it has a continuous power source, such as electricity from a battery or a power line.

AUTOMATED MACHINES IN THE MIDDLE AGES

After the fall of classical Greece and Rome, many Greek books made their way to the Middle East. They were studied by Arab scholars, who were inspired by the knowledge the books contained. Around 800 CE, the caliph of Baghdad commissioned the *Book of Ingenious Devices*, which collected all the Greek knowledge and writing about mechanical devices. It describes the construction of about one hundred mechanical devices, including an automated flute, which is considered to be the first programmable device because it could be set to play different tunes.

In 1206, Al-Jazari (1136–1206) wrote the Persian work *The Book of Knowledge of Ingenious Mechanical Devices*, which describes designs for air- and water-driven machines and automata. One example from the book is a device intended to dispense wine and water at parties.

This device included an automated servant girl, an automated horse and rider, and an automated serving man. In China and Japan inventors at the royal courts also produced a variety of automata, including birds, animals, and moving figures.

The Renaissance saw the dawning of a new interest in finding scientific rather than religious explanations for natural phenomena, and the sciences of mechanics and physics advanced from the fourteenth through eighteenth centuries. Knowledge of mechanics and physics was brought back to Europe in Arab texts, enabling the first steps toward creating true programmable devices to take place.

Programmable devices are machines that can run without human interference after being given a set of instructions.

Al-Jazari's Book of Knowledge of Ingenious Mechanical Devices *was divided into six sections on different types of devices, including this mechanical clock.*

THE GOLEM

THE CONCEPT OF A FULL-SCALE ARTIFICIAL MAN WAS FIRST DESCRIBED IN JEWISH FOLKLORE. THIS ARTIFICIAL MAN WAS CALLED THE GOLEM, AND THERE ARE SEVERAL VERSIONS OF ITS STORY. ONE OF THE MOST OFTEN RECOUNTED STORIES INVOLVES THE HEAD RABBI OF SIXTEENTH-CENTURY PRAGUE, A CITY THAT IS NOW THE CAPITAL OF THE CZECH REPUBLIC.

AS THE STORY GOES, THE RABBI CONSTRUCTED AN ARTIFICIAL MAN OF CLAY IN ORDER TO PROTECT THE JEWS WHO WERE BEING PERSECUTED BY THE LOCAL AUTHORITIES. THE GOLEM WAS BROUGHT TO LIFE BY WRITING THE NAME OF GOD, OR THE WORD *EMET* (HEBREW FOR "TRUTH" OR "REALITY"), ON ITS BODY. (IN SOME VERSIONS OF THE STORY, THE WORD IS WRITTEN ON A PIECE OF PAPER PLACED UNDER THE GOLEM'S TONGUE.) LIKE MODERN ROBOTS, THE GOLEM COULD NOT THINK ON ITS OWN BUT CARRIED OUT TASKS LITERALLY, ACCORDING TO THE INSTRUCTIONS IT WAS GIVEN. WHEN THE INTIMIDATED PRAGUE AUTHORITIES AGREED TO STOP THEIR PERSECUTION OF THE CITY'S JEWISH POPULATION, THE GOLEM WAS DEACTIVATED BY ERASING OR REMOVING THE WORD FROM THE GOLEM'S BODY.

Early machines were programmed mechanically. For example, imagine a music box that is wound up, causing a gear to turn, which makes a set of metal teeth contact different pins to produce various notes to play a song.

This music box could be programmed to play a different song by changing the settings of its pins.

RENAISSANCE ROBOTS

Italian artist and inventor Leonardo da Vinci (1452–1519) gained knowledge of the human body from anatomical studies. Around 1495, he combined this knowledge with information on mechanics from ancient Greek texts to design, and some say build, the first version of a robot. It was a robot knight dressed in armor.

Leonardo's robot was designed to sit up and move its head and limbs to the accompaniment of automated drums. Made of wood, metal, and leather, its parts were operated

Robots based on Leonardo da Vinci's drawings and notes are exhibited at the Anatomy of Robots exhibition in Sydney, Australia, in 2010.

by a series of cables, gears, and pulleys connected to a mechanical controller in its chest. The same general principles are applied today to move the head and limbs of humanoid robots, although the controller today would be electronic rather than mechanical.

Leonardo da Vinci was not the only person to build a robot during the Renaissance. In 1540, Gianello Torriano (1515–1585) built a mechanical woman that played the mandolin, and in 1772, P. Jacquet-Droz (1721–1790) built a mechanical child that could write on paper with a pen.

EARLY COMPUTERS

Robotics could not fully come into its own, however, until the development of the computer and its ability to store and process complex instructions. The first steps toward building a working computer occurred during the Renaissance as well.

In 1642 Blaise Pascal (1623–1662), for whom the computer language Pascal is named, designed the first machine to perform arithmetical functions, producing the first "computing" machine. It used a series of gears inscribed with numerals and a ratchet device. This device could increment a gear when it reached the digit 9, allowing the machine to perform addition and subtraction mechanically.

Gottfried Wilhelm Leibniz (1646–1716) invented a way to allow the automatic calculator to perform multiplication. He did this by using repeated addition to simulate multiplication. This principle was later used in electronic computers. Leibniz also suggested that using a two-digit system rather than a ten-digit system would make performing automated mathematical calculations easier. This approach was resisted by scientists of the time, but more than a century later George Boole (1815–1864) developed a two-digit system, called binary. Today, it forms the basis of processing by all modern computers.

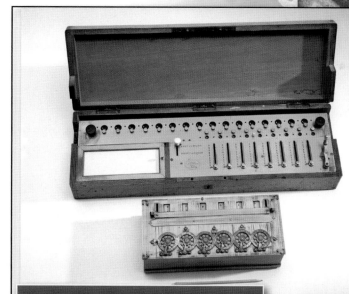

The calculating machine was invented by Blaise Pascal, France's most famous mathematician.

CHAPTER 2
The Birth of Electronics

During the nineteenth century, theories were developed that led to the creation of the electronic technology that makes modern-day robotics possible. This was the time of the Industrial Revolution, when machines began to replace individual craftsmen in the production of goods. As a result, factories became automated, allowing them to turn out goods in quantity. During this time, the first attempts were made to produce robots that could perform the work of human beings.

AUTOMATING FACTORIES

Today, robotics is closely associated with programming machines that can manipulate goods produced in factories. The roots of these industrial robots and the computers that control them can be traced to the early nineteenth century. During this time, steam engine technology reached a stage of development that made automated machines practical to use in factories.

As early as 1805, Joseph-Marie Jacquard (1752–1834) invented the first programmable automated production machine. He used a series of cards with holes punched through them to control the patterns made by an automatic loom used in textile production. Each hole or lack of hole in a card was read as "on" or "off" by the machine. This same type of binary punch card system would later be used to program early computers. Today's computers are programmed in the same manner at the most basic level, but the "on/off" signal is a "1" or "0" sent electrically, rather than a hole punched in a card.

The automated loom was invented by Joseph-Marie Jacquard. The loom could weave fabric automatically, producing a pattern controlled by punchcards.

THE BASIS OF ROBOTIC ELECTRONICS

English engineer Charles Babbage (1791–1871) wrote a paper in 1821 titled "Observations on the Application of Machinery to the Computation of Mathematical Tables." In it, he explained how it would be possible to construct a machine that could calculate astronomical tables automatically. He then set about building an example of the machine. Although his concept was sound, the difficulty of obtaining the necessary precision parts at that time kept him from completing the project. However, Babbage's "difference engine" is considered the first conceptualization of a computer.

The completed part of Charles Babbage's difference engine includes two thousand parts and still functions today. The numbers were represented on toothed wheels.

In 1877, William Thomson (1824–1907), Lord Kelvin, built the first practical computer. An avid yachtsman, he wished to calculate information about the tides. He figured out the formulas necessary to accomplish this, but the calculations were lengthy and time consuming. He believed it should be possible to build a machine to perform them instead of having to do so by hand. In 1876, using wires, pulleys, and dials, Thomson built a machine that, when a crank was turned, calculated the tides along the harbor. It could predict a year's worth of tides in four hours.

ROBOTS IN LITERATURE

THE FIRST MENTION OF ROBOTS IN LITERATURE MIGHT BE IN *THE ILIAD* BY HOMER. WHEN THE GOD HEPHAESTUS ENTERTAINS THE GODDESS THETIS IN HIS HOME, HOMER WRITES: "THERE WERE GOLDEN HANDMAIDS ALSO WHO WORKED FOR HIM, AND WERE LIKE REAL YOUNG WOMEN, WITH SENSE AND REASON, VOICE ALSO AND STRENGTH, AND ALL THE LEARNING OF THE IMMORTALS; THESE BUSIED THEMSELVES AS THE KING BADE THEM."

FROM THE NINETEENTH CENTURY THROUGH THE TWENTIETH CENTURY, ACTUAL ROBOTS HAVE APPEARED FREQUENTLY IN LITERATURE. HOWEVER, THE MODERN CONCEPT OF A ROBOT IS MORE CLOSELY ASSOCIATED WITH ISAAC ASIMOV THAN ANY OTHER WRITER. FROM THE 1940S ON, HE WROTE STORIES THAT FEATURED ROBOTS. HIS GREATEST CONTRIBUTION TO THE CONCEPT OF ROBOTS, HOWEVER, WAS HIS FORMULATION OF THE THREE LAWS OF ROBOTS IN HIS 1950 BOOK *I, ROBOT*.

1. A ROBOT MAY NOT HARM A HUMAN BEING, OR, THROUGH INACTION, ALLOW A HUMAN BEING TO COME TO HARM.

2. A ROBOT MUST OBEY THE ORDERS GIVEN TO IT BY HUMAN BEINGS, EXCEPT WHERE SUCH ORDERS WOULD CONFLICT WITH THE FIRST LAW.

3. A ROBOT MUST PROTECT ITS OWN EXISTENCE, AS LONG AS SUCH PROTECTION DOES NOT CONFLICT WITH THE FIRST OR SECOND LAW.

THE MECHANICAL WORKER

By the late nineteenth century, experiments began in creating "automated" workers. In 1868 engineers Zadoc P. Dederick and Isaac Grass created a steam-powered man who pulled a cart. This was followed by the development of steam-powered mechanical men of various sorts by a number of other inventors. One such inventor was George Moore of Canada. In 1893, he produced a steam-powered man who could walk at speeds of up to five miles per hour (eight kilometers per hour).

However, the advent of electricity as a practical source of power to run machines ended interest in steam-powered robots.

Robots perform many tasks on production lines. Although not human in form, they are a modern version of the mechanical worker.

CHAPTER 3
Cybernetics and Automation

A dvances in electronics, cybernetics, and computer science led to the creation of fully functional robots. Advances in electronics made it possible for control devices to use electrical signals to communicate with robots. Cybernetics is the technology of communicating with, and receiving feedback from, machines such as robots. Cybernetics allowed for the creation of more sophisticated robots that were better able to interact with their surroundings. Computer science encompasses the writing of computer software and algorithms to provide instructions to electronic machines such as robots. All three of these areas are key to the development of modern robots.

CYBERNETICS

Cybernetics enabled the development of advanced robots. This was the final stage in developing a modern "controller" for robotics. Today a controller is understood as a device that not only controls the speed, motion, and force of an automated machine, but also adjusts these factors in response to feedback from the robot. Feedback is registered by sensors that measure elements of the robot's performance such as direction, force, and speed, among other factors. This self-adjustment makes it possible for the robot to work without human intervention.

During the 1940s, mathematician Norbert Wiener (1894–1964) worked with engineer Julian Bigelow (1913–2003) to create control systems for antiaircraft guns. These guns had to be able to swivel to track the movement of passing planes. Wiener observed that, in order to control the movement of the guns' components, it was necessary for the system to have some means of feedback that would allow it to "know"

Professor Norbert Wiener, here at the Massachusetts Institute of Technology, is the founder of cybernetics.

which motion was occurring. This would allow the antiaircraft gun to adjust itself accordingly for different movements. In 1948 Wiener wrote a book called *Cybernetics: or the Control and Communication in the Animal and the Machine,* in which he presented the idea that one could simulate biological and social responses in inanimate objects by using sensors to provide feedback to machines.

Warren McCulloch (1893–1969), director of the Neuropsychiatric Institute at the University of Illinois, became interested in Wiener's ideas. He wanted to combine elements of neuroscience, mathematics, and engineering to create machine systems that could mimic human behavior. In 1952, McCulloch moved his research team to MIT to work on cybernetics. The basic areas of cybernetics were developed at MIT: machine perception, learning, memory, regulation, and adaptation. This research laid the foundation for artificial intelligence and modern robotics.

THE DEVELOPMENT OF THE COMPUTER

Cybernetics alone, however, would not allow the development of a machine that could emulate human capabilities and behavior. Modern robotics would not be possible without the computer. From the 1940s on, a series of advances took place that led to the development of modern electronic computers. The difference between mechanical and electronic computers is that an electronic computer uses an electrical signal rather than a mechanical device to change its switches to "on" or "off," allowing it to perform calculations.

Many of these advances were made during World War II and were funded with government money as a part of the war effort. Some of the earliest modern computers were designed by the Allies in order to crack German codes. In 1940 at Iowa State University, John Atanasoff (1903–1996) and Clifford Berry (1918–1963) developed the first true electronic computer, called the Atanasoff-Berry Computer, or ABC. During World War II, a group of British code breakers was charged with deciphering coded messages written by the Germans. The German code became known as the Enigma code, and they created it using a device called the Enigma machine. The British developed Heath Robinson, a code-breaking computer, and later in 1944 the first of the Colossus series of computers. These early computers could perform mathematical operations very fast, but they could not be programmed.

The development of ENIAC (Electronic Numerical Inegrator and Computer) was encouraged by the war effort during World War II.

In 1945, the Electronic Numerical Integrator and Computer, or ENIAC, was completed. ENIAC was the first programmable computer. It was designed by J. Presper Eckert (1919–1995) and John Mauchly (1907–1980) at the University of Pennsylvania Moore School of Electrical Engineering and funded by the U.S. Department of Defense. Unlike a computer that could merely be set up to run through a series of calculations faster than a human being could, ENIAC could use subroutines. By using subroutines, a computer can be programmed to perform different activities depending on the result of a calculation.

Computers in the 1940s were large and often occupied entire rooms. Today's computers use small computer chips that fit on circuit boards.

After completing the subroutine, the computer returns to the main program. This breakthrough significantly increased the processing ability of computers by allowing them to perform different functions according to the result of a given processing step.

METROPOLIS

ONE OF THE EARLIEST FILMS TO FEATURE ROBOTS IS *METROPOLIS*, MADE IN GERMANY IN 1927 AND DIRECTED BY FRITZ LANG. THE FILM CAPTURES THE PLIGHT OF EARLY TWENTIETH-CENTURY URBAN LABORERS WORKING ANONYMOUSLY IN FACTORIES AND THEIR FEAR OF BEING OPPRESSED AND DEHUMANIZED BY THOSE WHO HAVE MONEY AND POWER. IN IT, A DERANGED SCIENTIST CREATES A ROBOT, NAMED MARIA, TO BECOME THE REVOLUTIONARY LEADER OF THE WORKERS AND INCITE THEM TO VIOLENCE.

Mathematician John von Neumann (1903–1957) developed the concept of storing data and instructions in a computer's circuitry. He coined the term "memory" to describe this kind of data storage. Von Neumann's work became the basis for the Electronic Discrete Variable Computer (EDVAC) created at the University of Pennsylvania in 1951. It still forms the basis for how computers operate today.

In the mid-1950s, computer technology took a giant step forward with the development of the transistor. A transistor is a tiny piece of semiconducting material, such as silicon, with terminals attached to it that conduct electricity. Groups of transistors used together form an integrated circuit, more commonly called a computer chip. The development of technology to print microscopic circuits on silicon made it possible to string together a large number of circuits in a very small space, vastly increasing the processing capabilities of computers. Today computer chips are made by printing vast numbers of such circuits on a wafer of silicon that is cut into tiny pieces—hence the term "computer chip."

ADVANCES IN ROBOTIC AUTOMATION

One of the most influential people in the development of industrial robotics was George Devol (1912–), who created the first electronically controlled robotic arm in 1954. He also developed a magnetic recording system that could read instructions from a drum coated with magnetic material. This is the same basic principle used in the hard drives on computers today. In 1955, Devol and Joseph F. Engelberger (1925–) formed a company to manufacture commercial industrial robots. The company was called Unimation, or universal automation. Devol used the term "universal automation" to describe a type of robot that could be programmed to perform a variety of tasks.

CHAPTER 4
Artificial Intelligence

I n the mid-twentieth century, researchers began to develop techniques that would allow machines to learn and to mimic human responses. The goal was to create a machine that could not only perform a programmed task repeatedly but also learn and adapt so that it could perform more complex functions, similar to those performed by human workers. This mimicking of human thought was called artificial intelligence, or AI.

Machine learning is at the heart of artificial intelligence. Machine learning is based on the premise that every aspect of

Computer pioneer Alan Turing helped crack the German Enigma code during World War II. He described a "logical machine" in 1948, "the Turing machine."

learning can be formulated so precisely that a machine can simulate it. Artificial intelligence allows machines to acquire information, make decisions based on the accumulated information, and then produce output based on its decision.

THE EARLY YEARS OF AI

In 1937, British mathematician Alan Turing (1912–1954) proposed that a computer could perform any problem-solving or decision-making task a human being could. He developed the concept of a computer that could acquire knowledge the way a human being does. He also proposed that, if a human being engaged in a

MIT professor Rodney Brooks works with his artificially intelligent robot Cog, which is attempting to program and reprogram itself through interaction with people and objects.

"conversation" with a computer cannot tell whether he or she is conversing with a person or a machine, then the machine could be considered "intelligent." This has become known as the Turing Test. Turing's work spurred an interest in developing machines that could "think" like human beings.

In 1943 Warren McCulloch and Walter Pitts (1923–1969) developed a mathematical model of "neural net" computing. A neural net mimics the network of inter-linked neurons in the brain.

In an artificial neural network, processing elements, referred to as nodes, are linked together to form a net-work. The nodes work together to perform tasks. The more that given nodes are used together, the stronger their relationship becomes. The advantage of neural networks is that they allow the use of approximation, which lets a machine operate on incomplete data. For instance, a neural network computer can "estimate" a high likelihood that a certain action is correct or that a certain image represents a flaw in a component with-out having to be programmed to understand something that exactly matches what it encounters. In this way a neural network can simulate the way that human beings make judgments based on partial information.

THE LANGUAGE OF AI

New computer languages were invented to allow comput-ers to process information efficiently enough to make AI

A Real Thinking Machine

In 1993 the Humanoid Robotics Group at MIT, led by Rodney Brooks, started work on Cog (short for "cognition"), a robot that will learn the same way that a human being does. Cog will learn through interaction with its environment. Doing so requires the ability to perceive and draw conclusions, skills that are difficult to instill in a robot.

In order for Cog to interact with people, it is necessary to get people to interact with the robot. To this end, the lab is working on giving Cog a head with features that can convey expressions the way human faces do. This will ensure that people will interact with it naturally. The researchers are also trying to find a way to give Cog an understanding of social skills, which will allow it to interface naturally with people. According to Brian Scassellati of the Cog project, "Normal social interactions depend upon the recognition of other points of view, the understanding of other mental states, and the recognition of complex non-verbal signals of attention and emotional state." Therefore, the project must find a way to give Cog the ability to recognize and interpret these elements. The Cog project has a long way to go, but if the group succeeds, it would be the first step toward creating a true android—a humanoid robot that behaves like a human being.

possible. In 1959, John McCarthy (1927–) and Marvin Minsky (1927–) founded the AI lab at MIT, one of the facilities that has led artificial intelligence research. At the lab, McCarthy developed LISP, one of the first programming languages that could be used for AI. Using LISP, a computer searched a massive list of possible solutions to a problem repeatedly until it found the best one.

In the 1960s, AI researchers started work on developing "expert systems." This work, which has continued to the present day, is focused on accumulating large databases (repositories of data) on various subjects, such as medicine or geology, and developing rules that allow computers to make judgments about the information. These rules are intended to simulate the way in which human beings think.

The Strata Center at MIT includes the Laboratory for Computer Science, the Artificial Intelligence Laboratory, and the Laboratory for Information Decision Making.

CHAPTER 5
Mobile Robots

B y the mid-1960s interest was growing in creating freestanding robots. Stationary industrial robots are fine for factory use, but many people were interested in creating robots that could move about freely and perform tasks as needed. The first mobile robots were very basic. For example, one of the first mobile robots, Shakey, created at the Stanford Artificial Intelligence Laboratory between 1966 and 1972, consisted of a TV camera (for visual input) and remote links to computers, sensors, and a few other components mounted on a platform that rolled around on wheels. Shakey was able to navigate around an enclosed space by itself.

By 1984, the Stanford lab had become an independent entity, the Stanford Research Institute, and developed a robot called Flakey, which had stereo vision, a computer program that allowed it to interpret speech, and a sophisticated system of sensors that allowed it to receive information from its environment. Flakey could follow people around and use its speech recognition system to respond to spoken commands.

MODERN MOBILE ROBOTS

One of the big supporters of mobile robot development was the National Aeronautics and Space Administration

(NASA), which needed robots to explore the surfaces of planets. In 1966, the first robotic space explorer, *Surveyor*, landed on the moon. NASA continues to fund the development of mobile robots. In 2001, MD Robotics of Canada's Space Station Remote Manipulator System was launched to complete assembly of the International Space Station. In 2003, two NASA Mars rover robots landed on the surface of Mars. Designed with treads that would allow them to traverse uneven surfaces, the Mars rovers were equipped to gather geological information.

Another big impetus for the development of mobile robots came from the military. The military wanted to create robots that could go into enemy territory and move about intelligently on their own. These robots would be able to deliver supplies, provide

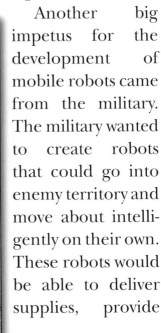

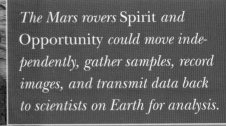

The Mars rovers Spirit *and* Opportunity *could move independently, gather samples, record images, and transmit data back to scientists on Earth for analysis.*

scouting information, and perform other missions. Beginning in 1984 the U.S. Department of Defense's Defense Advanced Research Projects Agency (DARPA) began to fund research into robotic automated land vehicles, or ALVs. Much like human drivers, these completely automated vehicles process visual information and use a variety of mapping systems to navigate roads and terrain. The earliest effort was NavLab, a Chevy van rigged with computer equipment.

One of the key scientists involved in the development of NavLab was William Red Whittaker, direc-

General Peter Schoonmaker, U.S. Army Chief of Staff, talks about military robots at a 2007 Senate Armed Services Committee hearing.

tor of Carnegie Mellon University's Field Robotics Center. Whittaker and his associates also built robots to work on the cleanup in the wake of the Three Mile Island nuclear power plant disaster in 1979 and the Chernobyl nuclear power plant disaster in Ukraine in 1986. In 1986, Whittaker founded his own company, RedZone

Robotics, Inc. Whittaker focused on the development of robots that could work in hazardous environments. Whittaker's teams at the Carnegie Mellon University field lab developed robots that have searched for meteorites in Antarctica and explored Mars's surface. In the 1990s, one of his teams developed a six-legged walking robot to explore the Mount Spurr volcano in Alaska.

In the twenty-first century, companies began working on mobile robots for personal use as well. Carnegie Mellon University's Robots and People team has been working on developing a service robot that can assist patients and the elderly. GeckoSystems' Mobile Service Robot line is also designed to help the elderly. Gecko's robots, called CareBots, can navigate independently and communicate verbally. In 2009, iRobot (maker of the vacuuming robot Roomba), established a health care unit to work on developing an eldercare robot.

In 2009, scientists at the Intel Lab at Carnegie Mellon University held a public demonstration of HERB, the House Exploring Robotic Butler. HERB is still a work in progress; the researchers are designing the robot so it will be able to analyze and navigate its environment, respond to commands, and manipulate objects, all without human intervention.

WALKING ON TWO LEGS

Ever since people first thought about building artificial versions of living organisms, they desired to make one in the form of a human being. One of the major problems with making a humanoid robot, however, is that it must walk on two legs. People must constantly adjust their bodies to maintain balance while moving. For a humanoid robot to function successfully, it would need to do the same. In 1970, a Serbian engineer, Miomir Vukobratovic, developed a concept to cope with this problem. He called it the Zero Moment Point, and it refers to the point at which the various forces that affect the robot's stability are in balance. Japanese scientists and engineers used this concept to pioneer humanoid robots.

In 1973 Ichiro Kato's bioengineering group at Waseda University in Japan created the first humanoid robot, Wabot-1. Wabot-1 had artificial eyes and ears and even an artificial mouth. It could

ASIMO, Honda's humanoid robot, can walk while holding hands with a person, run at 4 miles per hour (6 km per hour), carry objects, and run in a circular pattern.

communicate in Japanese and grasp objects with its hands, which were equipped with tactile sensors. In 1984, the same group produced Wabot-2, a robot that could play music. Wabot-2 could see the notes on a sheet of music, process this information, then play the notes, using its hands to play the keys of an electric organ and its feet to press the pedals of the instrument.

In February 2002, Honda's humanoid robot ASIMO rang the bell to open trading on the New York Stock Exchange in honor of the twentieth anniversary of the trading of Honda's stock on the exchange—and more than twenty years of Honda's working on creating a humanoid robot. According to Honda, "At the NYSE ceremony, the 4 foot ASIMO robot ascended a set of stairs on the bell podium, shook hands with NYSE Chairman and CEO Richard Grasso, rang the opening bell and waved and clapped along with hundreds of traders on the floor of the Exchange." Honda's ultimate goal is to create a robot that can move and behave just like a person in order to act as a service robot. Honda began its research efforts in 1986.

From 1987 to 1992, Honda worked on the E (for "experimental") series of robots. The company wanted to develop the technology that would make robots walk. In 1993, it began working on prototype bipedal robots, and in 1997, it debuted the P3, an independent 5-foot-tall (152-centimeters) walking robot.

HUMANOID ROBOTS IN THE HOME

IN A SURE SIGN THAT ROBOTS ARE MOVING INTO THE MAIN-STREAM, IN 2001 BOTH MATTEL AND HASBRO INTRODUCED ROBOTIC BABY DOLLS. THESE DOLLS CAN DO THINGS LIKE BLINK, CRY, AND SIMULATE SLEEP. THE TWO TOYMAKERS TOOK DIFFERENT APPROACHES TO THEIR DOLLS. HASBRO'S IS MORE SOPHISTICATED, BEING ABLE TO CALL, CRY, COO, AND EVEN MATURE. HOWEVER, IT LOOKS MORE LIKE A ROBOT THAN A LIVING BABY. MATTEL'S TOY IS MORE LIMITED IN WHAT IT CAN DO, BUT IT LOOKS LIKE A TRADITIONAL BABY DOLL. MATTEL'S DECISION TO GO FOR LESS ROBOTICS AND MORE HUMAN CHARACTERISTICS WAS THE RESULT OF STUD-IES WITH CHILDREN THAT SHOWED THAT THEY WANTED A DOLL THAT LOOKED HUMAN MORE THAN THEY WANTED ADDI-TIONAL FUNCTIONS. THIS BRINGS UP AN IMPORTANT POINT FOR THE FUTURE OF ROBOT DEVELOPMENT. WHILE MACHINE-LIKE ROBOTS MAY BE ADEQUATE FOR FACTORY USE, FOR A PERSONAL ROBOT, THE MORE HUMAN-LOOKING A ROBOT IS, THE MORE WIDELY ACCEPTED IT MAY BE.

The P3 represented a major advance in bipedal robots, but it still had to stop to negotiate challenges like mak-ing sharp turns. Honda's ASIMO robot, though, can walk continuously the way a human being does, using real-time feedback to guide its adjustments. Not to be outdone, Sony Corporation debuted the SDR-4X humanoid robot at the computer convention Robodex in 2003. The SDR-4X can sing and dance and even gave a performance at the convention.

NASA'S HUMANOID ROBOTS

In 1997, NASA began development work on Robonaut at the Dexterous Robot Lab at the Johnson Space Center in Houston, Texas. Robonaut, a legless humanoid robot, is intended to assist astronauts inside and outside space stations and vehicles. In 2010, NASA and General Motors jointly introduced Robonaut 2 (R2), a stronger and more versatile version of Robonaut. R2 can even use some tools used by human workers. "Working side by side with humans, or going where the risks are too great for people, machines like Robonaut will expand our capability for construction and discovery," Mike Coats, the director of the Johnson Space Center, said in a statement on the NASA R2 Web site.

We have not yet reached the point where robots look and perform like people, but all the inventions and technologies discussed in this book have contributed to progress in this direction. There is little doubt that as we progress through the twenty-first century, researchers will move ever closer to the creation of a fully functional humanoid robot.

INTERVIEW WITH ROBOTICIST
GAIL DRAKE

GAIL DRAKE IS A TECHNOLOGY TEACHER AT BATTLEFIELD HIGH SCHOOL IN HAYMARKET, VIRGINIA. THE SCHOOL ASKED HER TO START A FIRST ROBOTICS TEAM. HERE'S HER INTERVIEW:

PRIOR TO BECOMING A HIGH SCHOOL TEACHER, I WAS A PROFESSIONAL IN INFORMATION TECHNOLOGY AND A PROFESSOR. MY DECISION TO MOVE TO HIGH SCHOOL HAD TWO COMPONENTS: I LOVE TO TEACH, AND I LOVE TO WORK WITH PEOPLE ON BEING THE BEST THEY CAN BE.

IN NOVEMBER OF THE SECOND YEAR OF BATTLEFIELD HIGH SCHOOL BEING OPEN, I WAS CONTACTED BY THE SCHOOL BOARD. THE BOARD HAD A REQUEST FROM A LOCAL CORPORATION FOR THE SCHOOL DISTRICT TO START A FIRST ROBOTICS TEAM. IN SIX WEEKS WE STARTED A TEAM, AND THE GAME RULES WERE ANNOUNCED ON THE FIRST SATURDAY OF THE CALENDAR YEAR.

DURING THE SEASON, THE LEVEL OF LEARNING THAT WAS TAKING PLACE, THE LEVEL OF DEDICATION TO THE END GOAL BY STUDENTS AND ADULTS ALIKE, WAS AT THE HIGHEST LEVELS I HAD EVER EXPERIENCED. THIS PARALLELED WHAT I FELT WAS IMPORTANT IN LIFE, AND WHERE I WANTED TO MAKE A DIFFERENCE. I HAVE DONE FIRST EACH YEAR SINCE.

IN YOUR OPINION, WHAT ARE SOME OF THE MOST EXCITING THINGS HAPPENING IN THE WORLD OF ROBOTICS RIGHT NOW?

SOME OF THE MOST EXCITING ROBOTS ARE THOSE CREATED TO SAVE LIVES OR FUNCTION IN DANGEROUS SITUATIONS.

For instance, the robot submarines used to cap the pipe in the [BP] Gulf oil spill, robots that assist police through surveillance and bomb disabling, and military robots such as UAVs. It has also been fascinating to see the development of manufacturing, farming, and medical robots.

WILL PEOPLE EVER HAVE ROBOTS IN THEIR HOMES?

People already do have robots in their homes! The company iRobot sells robots that vacuum the floors, wash the floors, sweep the garage, clean the pool, clean the gutters, and cut the lawn. (However, a different robot is needed to perform all of these functions.) Probotics, Inc. has a robot that will move objects from one location to another. The prediction is that robots will exist in the home, but each will perform a specific task. We may never see an android that can accomplish all of the tasks performed by humans.

WHAT KINDS OF ETHICAL AND LEGAL QUESTIONS WILL THE ROBOTS OF THE FUTURE POSE?

My son discusses this with me often. How can we hold a robot to laws? Who is really held accountable? What would it matter if you placed a robot in jail? Or destroyed it? Is it the person behind the robot that matters, and is it hard to control who is allowed to create a robot?

IN YOUR OPINION, WHAT IS THE DIRECTION THAT ROBOTICS WILL TAKE IN THE FUTURE? WILL INTELLIGENT HUMANOID ROBOTS EXIST?

THE CURRENT FOCUS OF ROBOTS IS TO CREATE ROBOTS THAT PERFORM ONE TASK, OR A SMALL NUMBER OF TASKS. I BELIEVE WE WILL SEE ROBOTICS INTEGRATED INTO EVERYDAY ELECTRONICS.

I BELIEVE THAT SWARM ROBOTICS WILL CONTINUE TO BE DEVELOPED IN THE FUTURE. NANOROBOTICS (OR THE CREATION OF EXTREMELY TINY ROBOTS) IS CURRENTLY IN THE RESEARCH PHASE, AND I BELIEVE IT WILL CONTINUE UNLESS IT IS DETERMINED THAT THEY WILL NOT BE COST EFFECTIVE TO PRODUCE.

I HOPE THAT INTELLIGENT HUMANOID ROBOTS WILL NOT EXIST. I FEEL THAT THE UNITED STATES WILL NOT TAKE THE LEAD ON THIS ONE. WE ARE, HOWEVER, PLACING VALUE ON ARTIFICIAL INTELLIGENCE IN ROBOTICS, I.E., ROBOTS THAT CAN REPLICATE HUMAN INTELLIGENCE.

GLOSSARY

algorithm A mathematical rule used in computer programming.

android A robot that looks like a human being.

appendage A limb, real or artificial.

automaton A machine that looks and acts like a human being.

binary system A mathematical system that uses two states (on or off; 0 or 1) to encode data and instructions used by a computer.

caliph A title given to medieval Muslim rulers of Baghdad.

compound pulley A combined fixed and movable pulley.

entities Physical beings.

humanoid Having the shape of a human being.

inanimate Not living.

mechanics A branch of science that deals with the movement of objects.

physics A branch of science that deals with the physical properties of objects and the forces that act on them.

piston A mechanical component that consists of a disk or cylinder that fits tightly in a cylindrical casing and pumps air or fluids.

ratchet A mechanical component that moves other components up and down in steps.

semiconductor A material that conducts electricity but does so less well than metal.

sensor A device that is sensitive to sound, light, pressure, or other physical characteristics. Sensors send signals to a monitoring or controlling device.

simulate To imitate or model.

FOR MORE INFORMATION

American Nuclear Society: Robotics and Remote Systems
555 North Kensington Avenue
La Grange Park, IL 60526
(800) 323-3044
Web site: http://www.ans.org
This organization sponsors a student conference and
    provides grants to students to encourage their inter-
    est and involvement in developing robots for work in
    hazardous environments.

Association of Computer Machinery (ACM)
2 Penn Plaza, Suite 701
New York, NY 10121-0701
(800) 342-6626
Web site: http://www.acm.org
The ACM runs special-interest groups that work on spe-
    cific areas of computer science, including robotics.

FIRST Robotics Canada
Richard Yasui
FIRST Robotics Administrator
Toronto District School Board
140 Borough Drive, Level 1
Toronto, ON M1P 4N6
Canada
(416) 396-5907
Web site: http://www.firstroboticscanada.org
This organization sponsors robotics competitions for
    students at schools throughout Canada.

Institute of Electrical and Electronics Engineers:
   Robotics and Automation Society
1828 L Street NW, Suite 1202
Washington, DC 20036-5104
(800) 678-4333
Web site: http://www.ieee-ras.org
This organization provides information for students in
   computer and technology fields, including robotics.

The Robotics Institute
Carnegie Mellon University
5000 Forbes Avenue
Pittsburgh, PA 15213-3890
(412) 268-3818
Web site: http://www.ri.cmu.edu
This educational institution sponsors events that are
   open to the public and provides online information
   on research into robotics.

WEB SITES

Due to the changing nature of Internet links, Rosen
Publishing has developed an online list of Web sites
related to the subject of this book. This site is updated
regularly. Please use this link to access the list:

http://www.rosenlinks.com/robo/rth

FOR FURTHER READING

Angelo, Joseph A. *Robot Spacecraft.* New York, NY: Facts On File, 2006.

Asimov, Isaac. *I, Robot.* New York, NY: Spectra, 2008.

Čapek, Karel. *R.U.R.* New York, NY: Penguin Books, 2004.

Cook, David. *Robot Building for Beginners.* Berkeley, CA: Apress, 2010.

Dick, Phillip. *Do Androids Dream of Electric Sheep?* New York, NY: Oxford University Press, 2007.

Domaine, Helena. *Robotics.* Minneapolis, MN: Lerner Books, 2005.

Henderson, Harry. *Modern Robotics: Building Versatile Machines.* New York, NY: Chelsea House, 2007.

Ichibah, Daniel. *Robots from Science Fiction to Technological Revolution.* New York, NY: Harry Abrams, 2005.

Jefferis, David. *Robot Workers.* New York, NY: Crabtree, 2006.

Jones, David. *Mighty Robots: Mechanical Marvels that Fascinate and Frighten.* Toronto, ON: Annick Press, 2005.

Miller, Michael. *Absolute Beginner's Guide to Computer Science.* New York, NY: Que Publishing/Pearson Technology, 2009.

National Geographic. *Robots to Motorized Monocycles.* Washington, DC: National Geographic, 2009.

Piddock, Charles. *National Geographic Investigates: Future Tech: From Personal Robots to Motorized Monocycles.* Washington, DC: National Geographic, 2009.

Whitby, Blay. *Artificial Intelligence.* New York, NY: Rosen Publishing, 2009.

White, Steve. *Military Robots.* Danbury, CT: Children's Press, 2007.

Wright, Thomas R. *Manufacturing and Automation Technology.* Trinley Point, IL: Goodheart & Wilcox, 2004.

BIBLIOGRAPHY

Ashliman, D. L. "The Golem: A Jewish Legend." Retrieved March 2, 2010 (http://www.pitt.edu/~dash/golem.html).

Kurweil, Raymond. "The Age of Intelligent Machines, Chapter Five: Mechanical Roots." KurzweilAI.net. Retrieved March 2, 2010 (http://www.kurzweilai.net/articles/art0314.html?printable=1).

Marketing Week. "Mattel Launches Miracles Moves Robot Doll a Year Behind Schedule." March 1, 2001. Retrieved March 7, 2010 (http://www.marketingweek.co.uk/home/mattel-launches-miracle-moves-robot-doll-a-year-behind-schedule/2033735.article).

Massachusetts Institute of Technology. "Cog." Retrieved March 8, 2010 (http://www.ai.mit.edu/projects/humanoid-robotics-group/cog).

National Science Foundation. "HERB, the Robot Butler." February 1, 2010. Retrieved March 1, 2010 (http://www.nsf.gov/news/special_reports/science_nation/robotbutler.jsp).

Nocks, Lisa. *The Robot: The Life Story of a Technology.* Baltimore, MD: Johns Hopkins University Press, 2008.

Rosheim, Mark E. "Leonardo's Lost Robot." Institute and Museum of the History of Science. Retrieved February 28, 2010 (http://brunelleschi.imss.fi.it/genscheda.asp?appl=LIR&indice=63&xsl=sezione&lingua=ENG&chiave=100955).

Russell, Stewart. *Artificial Intelligence: A Modern Approach.* Upper Saddle River, NJ: Prentice Hall, 2009.

Waseda University Humanoid Robot Institute. "Wabot." Retrieved March 7, 2010 (http://www.humanoid.waseda.ac.jp/booklet/kato_2.html).

INDEX

ABOUT THE AUTHOR

Jeri Freedman has a B.A. degree from Harvard University. For fifteen years she worked for companies involved in cutting-edge technologies. She is the author of more than thirty young adult nonfiction books, including *Careers in Computer Technology: Computer Science and Programming, Digital Career Building Through Skinning and Modding*, and *Cyber Citizenship and Cyber Safety: Intellectual Property*.

PHOTO CREDITS

Cover Spencer Rowell/Taxi/Getty Images; cover (background), book art, back cover © Axel Lauerer/ Flickr/Getty Images; p. 7 © Bildarchiv Preussischer Kulturbesitz/Art Resource, NY; p. 9 © Science Source/ Photo Researchers; p. 11 Greg Wood/AFP Photo/Getty Images; pp. 13, 15, 16 SSPL/Getty Images; p. 18 Andrew Sacks/Riser/Getty Images; p. 20 Alfred Eisenstaedt/Pix, Inc./Time & Life Pictures/Getty Images; p. 22 MPI/ Getty Images; p. 23 Shutterstock; p. 26 Life Magazine/ Time & Life Pictures/Getty Images; p. 27 Ted Thai/Time & Life Pictures/Getty Images; p. 30 © Richard Sobol/ Zuma Press; p. 32 NASA/JPL/Cornell University/Mass Digital; p. 33 Karen Bleier/AFP/Getty Images; p. 35 Koichi Kamoshida/Getty Images.

Designer: Matthew Cauli; Editor: Nicholas Croce; Photo Researcher: Mary Levick